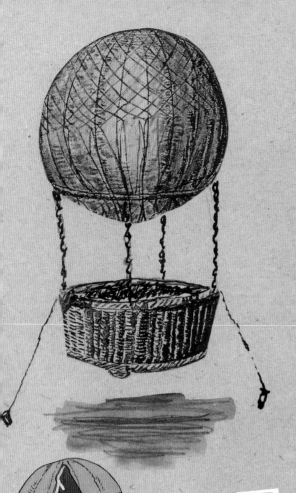

A IS FOR AUCKLAND

Diane Newcombe & Melissa Anderson Scott

RANDOM HOUSE
NEW ZEALAND

To BEAU,
CHRISTOPHER &
DEKLYN.....
KEEP READING!!
Melissa Anderson Scott

Bb

TE
HENGA

anawhata

PIHA

KAREKARE
BEACH

Whatipu

manukau entrance

SOUTH HEAD →

BIG BAY

GRAHAM'S
BEACH

blissful...........

basking...

MUSEUM

midnight...

Mm

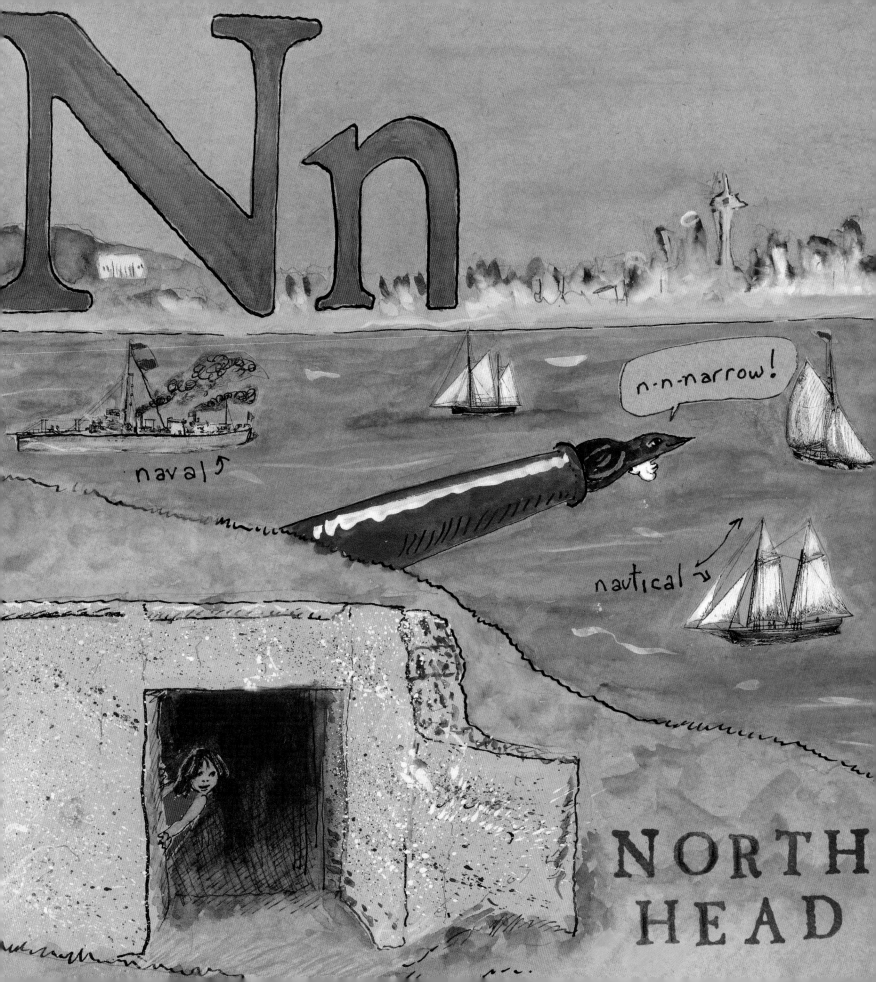

Pacific Events Centre

RANGITOTO

SKYTOWER
at sunset

S s

Uu

udder
underneath

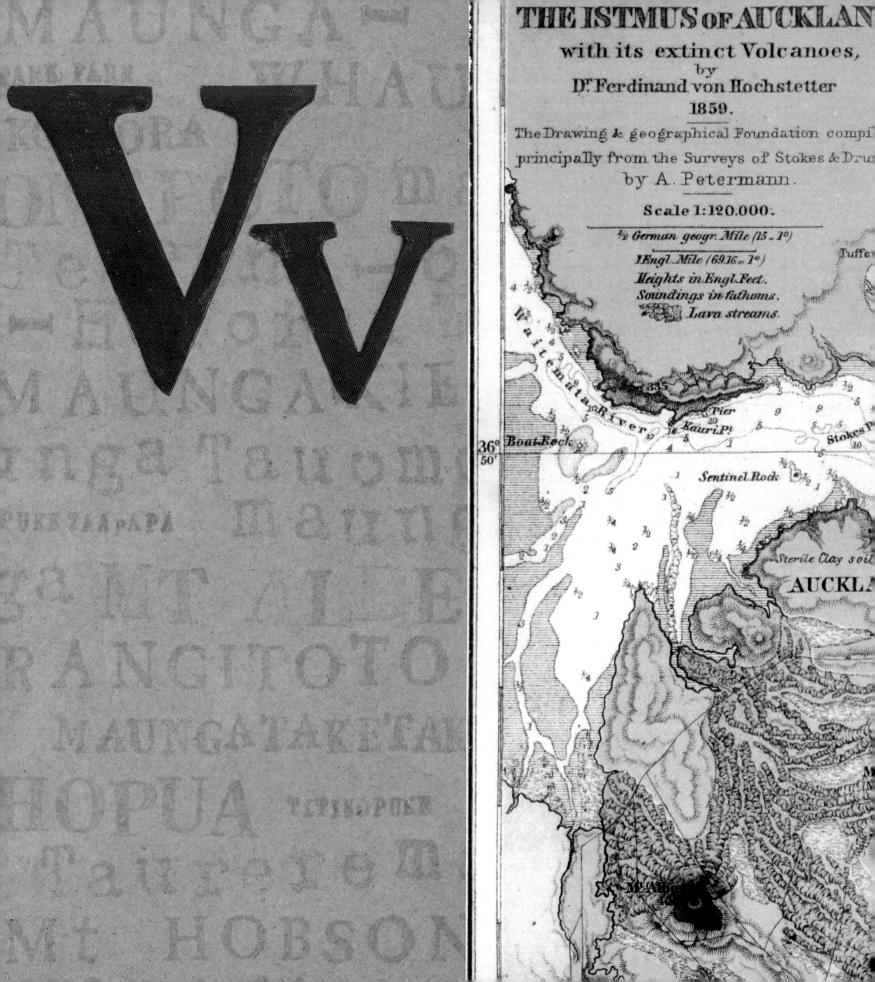

AUCKLAND
ZOO

z-z-z-z

AUCKLAND

Auckland, or Tamaki Makaurau, was settled by Maori hundreds of years ago, as it provided a strategic location on a narrow isthmus between two harbours. European settlement began around 1800, and Auckland was the capital of New Zealand from 1840 until 1865, when central government moved to Wellington. In November 2010, several cities and local councils of the Auckland region combined to become Auckland – All Around!

BEACHES AND BAYS

Auckland has three major harbours: Waitemata, Manukau and Kaipara. It also has coastlines on the Pacific Ocean and Tasman Sea, and dozens of islands. No wonder Aucklanders love heading off to beaches and bays by boat, bike or bus.

CIVIC

Built in 1929, the Civic Theatre is now owned by the people of Auckland and is one of only seven 'atmospheric' theatres in the world. Its gorgeous décor includes an Indian-inspired foyer and an auditorium of Middle Eastern fantasy design.

DUDER REGIONAL PARK

Twenty-three splendid regional parks are located all around Auckland. Duder Regional Park is situated on the Whakakaiwhara Peninsula, in the eastern part of Franklin. In the 14th century, this was the first place in the Waitemata Harbour to be visited by the Tainui canoe. After being settled first by Maori, then Europeans, it is now a place where all Aucklanders and visitors can explore, swim and walk.

EDEN PARK

It's hard to believe that New Zealand's biggest stadium, which is so near the city centre, used to be a swamp. It was drained in 1900 and since then has hosted many of New Zealand's biggest sporting events, including the 2011 Rugby World Cup final, when 61,000 people watched the All Blacks win against France.

FO GUANG SHAN TEMPLE

The Fo Guang Shan temple in the Auckland suburb of Flat Bush is a large and impressive temple and community centre of the Fo Guang Shan Buddhist movement.

GOAT ISLAND

Goat Island, situated north-east of Warkworth, is called Te Hawere-a-Maki in Te Reo Maori. It is part of the Hauraki Gulf Marine Reserve, New Zealand's first marine reserve, and so is a great place to see fish (they know they are safe here from the thousands of Aucklanders who go fishing). We wonder what the fish think of the thousands of visitors!

HARBOUR BRIDGE

The Harbour Bridge was built in 1959 with four lanes, and had four more lanes added 10 years later. Some days more than 200,000 cars cross over!

IHUMATAO AND INTERNATIONAL AIRPORT

Ihumatao, the ancestral home of the Wai o Hua iwi, is a large coastal area near Mangere. Here you can see large remnants of fossilised tree trunks dating back some 20,000 years on the shore at low tide, and the Otuataua Stonefields, an important archaeological site. And . . . Ihumatao has been the site of Auckland's International Airport since 1966. (Auckland also has many smaller places to land a plane: Ardmore and Dairy Flat on the mainland and on Waiheke and Great Barrier Islands.)

JELLICOE PARK

Jellicoe Park in Onehunga was established in 1882 and is one of Auckland's oldest parks. People come to enjoy swimming, walking in the gardens, and learning about our history. The Blockhouse built here in 1860 is an old defence post and is evidence of the land wars between local Maori and colonial troops.

K (KARANGAHAPE) ROAD

The Maori name Karangahape has been in use for well over 100 years. Of the many interpretations of its meaning, 'winding ridge of human activity' seems to be a very appropriate description for this inner-city road.

LION ROCK

Lion Rock is also known as Te Piha, the name now given to the west coast beach where it is situated. The rock itself is an eroded 16-million-year-old volcanic outcrop, which resembles a large male lion lying down. When you're at Lion Rock, remember to look out for lifeguards and listen to what they say!

MUSEUM

The Auckland War Memorial Museum is in the Auckland Domain on the dormant volcano named Pukekawa. The museum was built here in 1929 with money raised by Aucklanders in remembrance of those who died at war. It tells the story of Aotearoa New Zealand, its people, and its place in the Pacific.

NORTH HEAD

North Head (Maungauika) was one of a number of defence forts that were rapidly set up in the late 1800s to defend Auckland from a feared Russian attack. The fort was later expanded as part of Auckland's coastal defence system during the First and Second World Wars. A complex of tunnels, guns, searchlights and other fortifications make this a fascinating area to explore.

OTARA MARKET

Auckland is the largest Pacific city in the world! Come to the Otara Market on a Saturday morning and experience aspects of the Pacific such as music, food, produce and craft.

POU KAPUA

The Pou Kapua taonga ('treasure') is the largest totem of its type in the world, carved from a magnificent ancient kauri tree from the forests of the Te Rarawa iwi. It stands more than 20 metres high beside the Vodafone Events Centre in Manukau. See the website of Pou Kapua Creations (www.poukapua.com) for details of the Maori, Pacific and other indigenous carvers and artists who took part in the creation of Pou Kapua.

QUEEN STREET

Queen Street, in the city centre, was named after Queen Victoria, who was the reigning British monarch when Europeans (mostly from Britain) started settling in the area. There are several other 'Queen Streets' in the greater Auckland area, in suburbs which were separate towns before they were absorbed by the growing city. Check these out at Northcote, Otahuhu, Papakura, Pukekohe, Riverhead, Waiuku and Warkworth.

RANGITOTO

Rangitoto, an island in the Hauraki Gulf of the Waitemata Harbour, is the youngest of Auckland's volcanoes and was formed through violent eruptions about 600 years ago. The other major Gulf islands are Great Barrier (Aotea), Waiheke, Little Barrier (Hauturu), Kawau, Motuihe, Motutapu, Pakatoa, Rakino, Browns (Motukorea) and Tiritiri Matangi.

SKY TOWER

Sky Tower is the second tallest building in the southern hemisphere and is Auckland's primary FM radio transmitter. People bungy jump off it and run up all of its 1103 steps for special events.

TE HANA

Te Hana, situated on the upper reaches of the Kaipara Harbour, is the northernmost town in Auckland and is the home of the Te Hana Te Ao Marama Maori cultural centre.

UNDULATING HILLS

Can you imagine having lots of cows in a city? You can in a super city! The beautiful countryside areas of Rodney and Franklin are now part of Auckland, making it a town and country kind of place.

VOLCANOES

If you live in Auckland there's a possibility you live somewhere near or even on a volcano, as there are dozens around! Volcanoes were important sites of early Maori occupation, being ideal for fortified villages (pa), and now they add spectacular interest and views. They are mostly monogenetic, which means it is unlikely that any of the existing volcanoes will erupt again in the same place.

WAITAKERES

The Waitakere Ranges Regional Park includes more than 16,000 hectares of native rainforest and coastline. Its 250 kilometres of walking and tramping tracks provide access to beaches, breath-taking vistas, spectacular rocky outcrops, streams, waterfalls and farms which overlook the wild west coast.

X MARKS THE SPOT

There are around 1.5 million people living in Auckland - are you one of them? Can you mark where you live with an X? And more than 1.5 million people also visit Auckland every year - are you one of them? Can you mark your favourite place with an X? Where do you want to go next?

YES TO AUCKLAND ALL AROUND!

Aucklanders enjoy parades, for example on Anzac Day (25 April) when we are reminded of the tragedy of war, and also Santa Parades (just for fun). Wouldn't it be great to have one big 'Y' parade to celebrate being in Auckland?

ZOO

The Auckland Zoo at Western Springs covers 16 hectares and is home to 700 creatures. They might want to celebrate living in such a zippy zoo!

A RANDOM HOUSE BOOK published by Random House New Zealand
18 Poland Road, Glenfield, Auckland, New Zealand
For more information about our titles go to www.randomhouse.co.nz

A catalogue record for this book is available from the National Library of New Zealand
Random House New Zealand is part of the Random House Group
New York   London   Sydney   Auckland   Delhi   Johannesburg

First published 2013
© 2013 Diane Newcombe and Melissa Anderson Scott
The moral rights of the authors have been asserted

ISBN 978 1 77553 558 4

Map pages 36-37 courtesy of Sir George Grey Special Collections, Auckland Libraries (NZ Map 56946)
Design: Melissa Anderson Scott and Megan van Staden

Printed in China through Asia Pacific Offset Ltd